The Secret Subway

WRITTEN BY
SHANA COREY

ILLUSTRATED BY
RED NOSE STUDIO

schwartz & wade books · new york

Welcome to New York City—

the greatest city on earth!

You say it looks crowded? Dirty? DISGUSTING?

    The streets are filled with GARBAGE?

    Well . . . you're right.

    See, back in the 1860s, when this story
begins, there were no subways here, only
cobblestone streets.

    Pushcarts and wagons rocked and rumbled.

Stagecoaches and buggies jounced and jumbled.
Horses kicked up dirt and drivers shouted to be
heard. People pressed their way through it all, trying
not to get run over.

And it just kept getting worse.

Something had to be done!

From politicians to peddlers, street sweepers to scientists, everyone had ideas. "Why not make a moving street, so we can get wherever we want just by standing still?"

"What about building double-decker roads?"

"Or a railway on stilts?"

But no matter how much everyone talk-talk-TALKED, nothing ever seemed to get off the ground.

Then one day, high above it all, a man named Alfred Ely Beach stared down at the traffic and had an idea of his own.

Beach was a THINKER—a publisher and an inventor. His father had owned a newspaper, and Beach had grown up in a simmering soup of letters and words and newfangled notions. He was also a man of ACTION. And if there was one thing he loved more than thinking up ideas, it was making them happen. As Beach studied the street below, the wheels in his brain turned.

What if he built a train powered by an enormous
fan? he wondered. It would travel underground, where there
was no traffic or trash or weather to worry about. People
would get where they needed to go as if by magic!

Beach couldn't wait to get started. He was certain his
train could take New York into the future.

But there was a ROADBLOCK. The streets didn't belong to him. And since this would be a great big, messy, complicated job, permission to tunnel under them would not come easily.

So Beach hatched a sneaky plan. He would propose building an underground tube to carry mail instead. It wouldn't be that big. It wouldn't be that messy. It wouldn't be that complicated. No one could object.

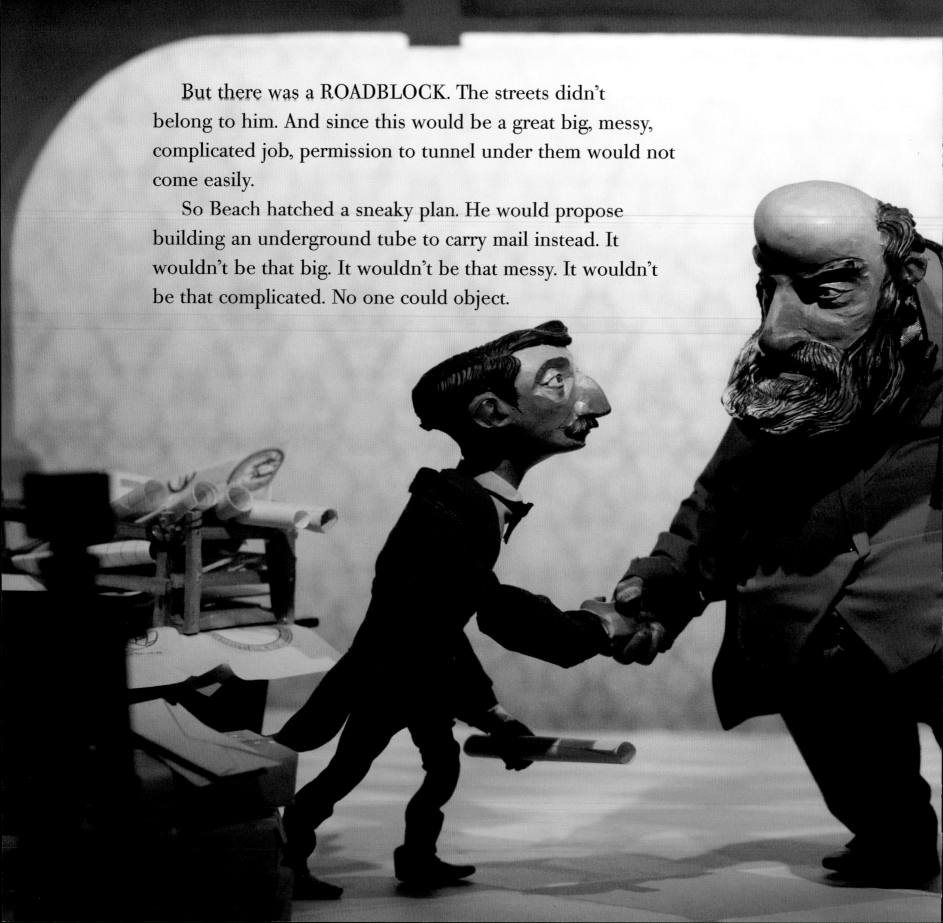

"A mail tube? Why not?" people said.
Even Boss Tweed agreed. (See, Boss Tweed
ran New York City—unofficially, that is.)
Beach got permission, but . . .

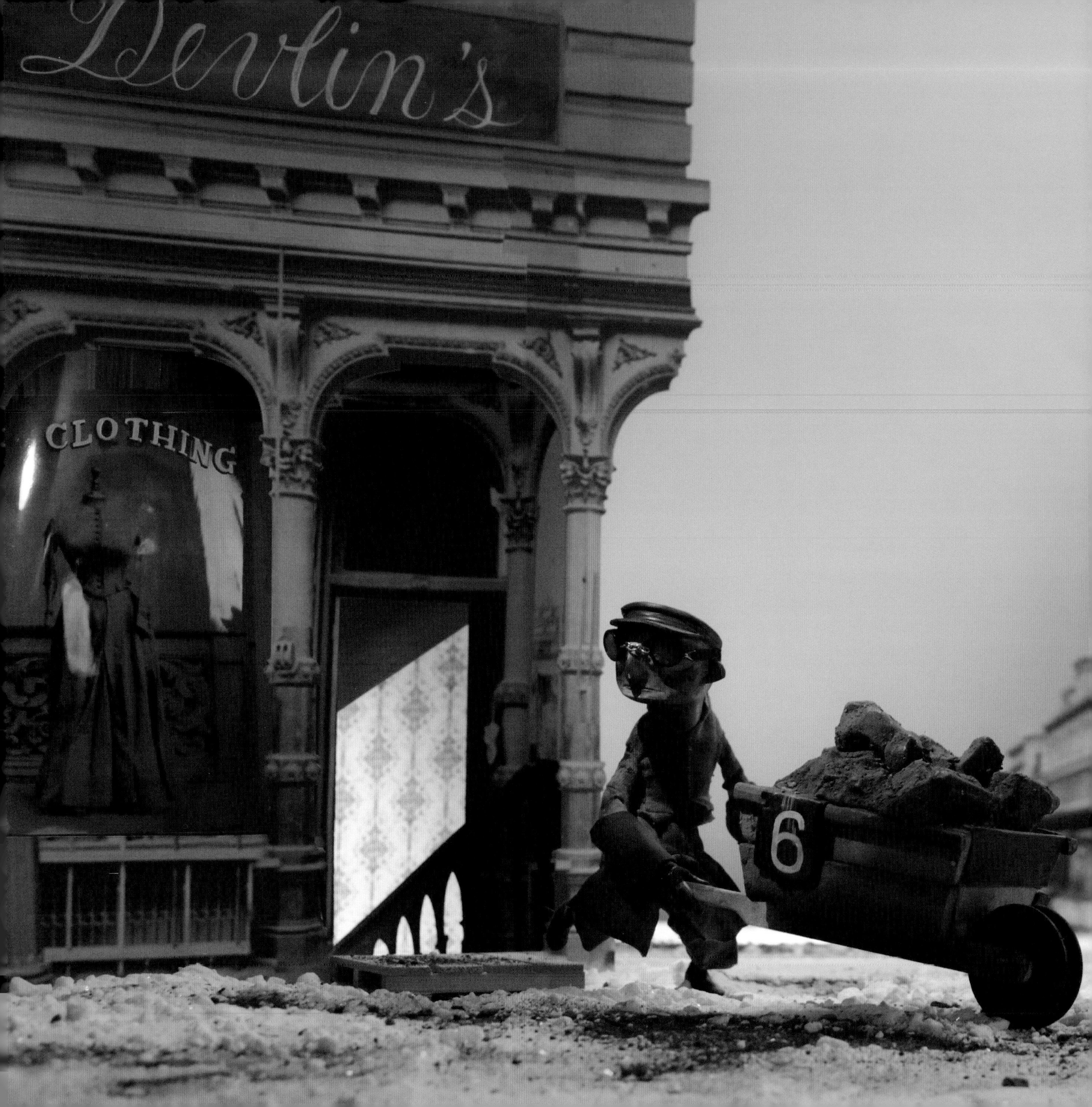
Devlin's
CLOTHING
6

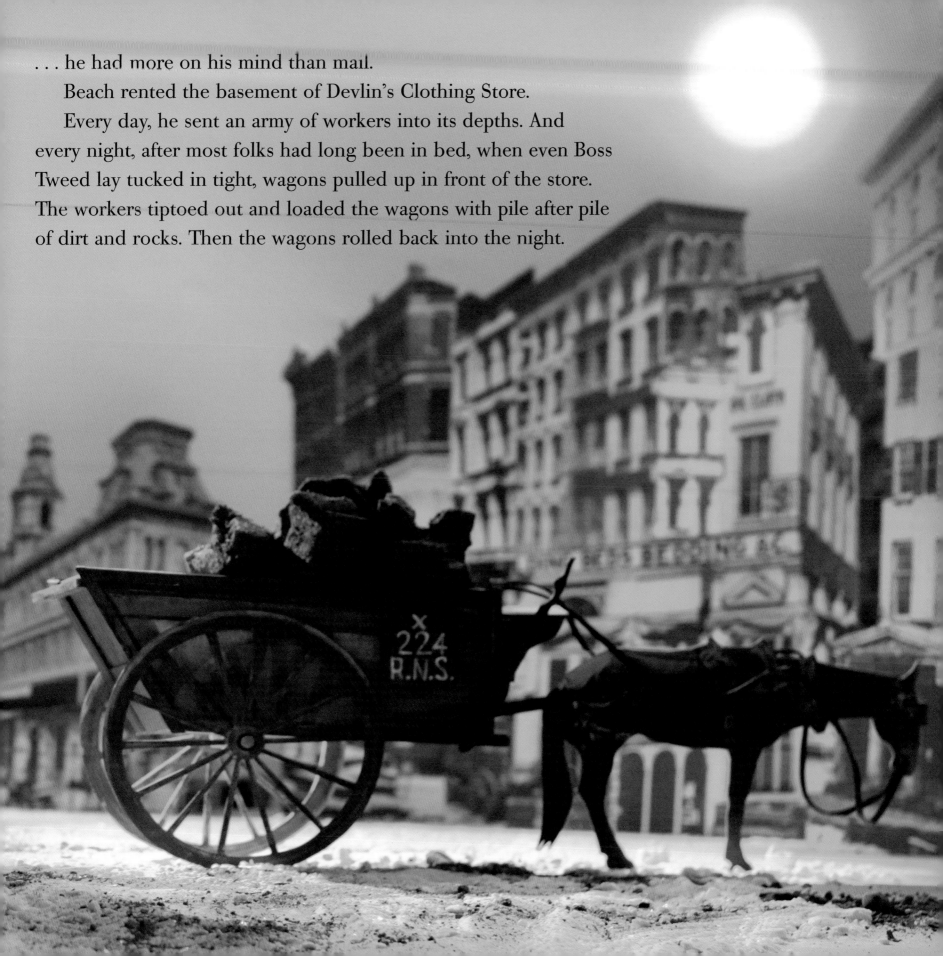

. . . he had more on his mind than mail.

Beach rented the basement of Devlin's Clothing Store.

Every day, he sent an army of workers into its depths. And
every night, after most folks had long been in bed, when even Boss
Tweed lay tucked in tight, wagons pulled up in front of the store.
The workers tiptoed out and loaded the wagons with pile after pile
of dirt and rocks. Then the wagons rolled back into the night.

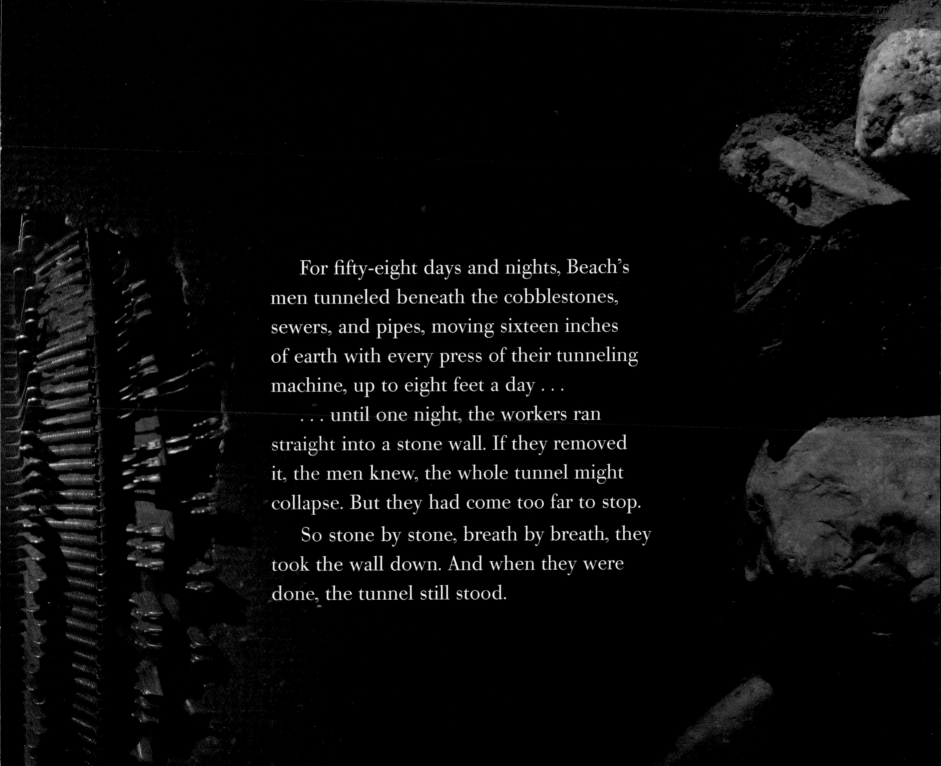

For fifty-eight days and nights, Beach's
men tunneled beneath the cobblestones,
sewers, and pipes, moving sixteen inches
of earth with every press of their tunneling
machine, up to eight feet a day . . .

. . . until one night, the workers ran
straight into a stone wall. If they removed
it, the men knew, the whole tunnel might
collapse. But they had come too far to stop.

So stone by stone, breath by breath, they
took the wall down. And when they were
done, the tunnel still stood.

Then one night, the drilling stopped. The tunnel—8 feet across and 294 feet long (big enough to hold a train full of people!), lined with brick and iron—was complete.

Now a new army of workers arrived carrying paintbrushes and plaster, curtains and mirrors.

When they were done, Devlin's basement resembled a fairyland.

Perfect! thought Alfred Ely Beach.

It was time to share his secret.

A few days later, distinguished citizens, reporters, and government officials all over New York opened their mail and found an invitation:

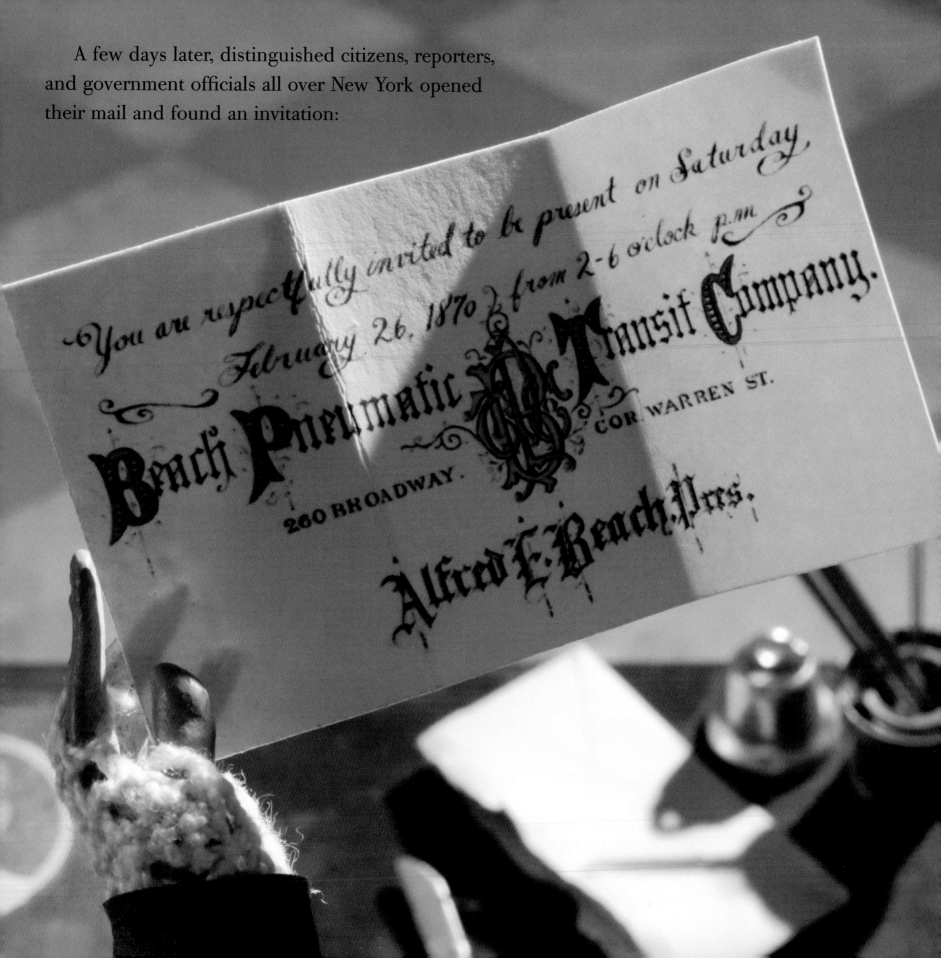

You are respectfully invited to be present on Saturday, February 26, 1870, from 2-6 o'clock p.m.

Beach Pneumatic Transit Company.

260 BROADWAY.

COR. WARREN ST.

Alfred E. Beach, Pres.

At precisely two o'clock on
February 26, Beach's guests left the
city streets and descended into Devlin's.
Then, one by one, they entered Beach's
spectacular subterranean waiting room.

Beach had thought of everything!
Gaslights glowed, illuminating paintings and
flowers and a fountain that glittered with
goldfish. A grandfather clock rang in the
hour, and a grand piano played. There was
even a tasty lunch spread out on a table.

The guests followed Beach down
six more steps onto a train platform.
A single car waited on the tracks.

"Remarkable!" marveled one reporter.

"The railroad of the future," agreed another.

"The problem of tunneling Broadway has
been solved!" cheered the newspapers.

That first day, guests simply admired the
train. But it wasn't long before the tunnel was
opened to the public and throngs of visitors
climbed aboard. With a flourish, an engineer
turned on the great fan. Then, *SWOOSH!*
A blast of air pushed the train down the tracks.

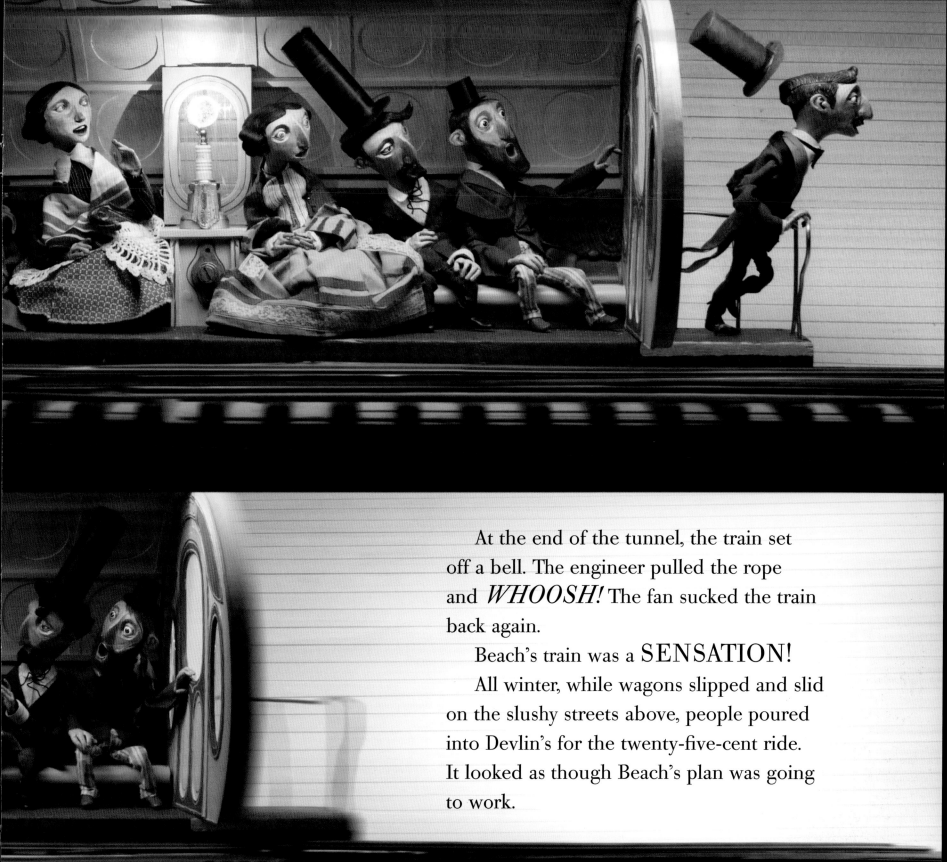

At the end of the tunnel, the train set
off a bell. The engineer pulled the rope
and *WHOOSH!* The fan sucked the train
back again.

Beach's train was a SENSATION!

All winter, while wagons slipped and slid
on the slushy streets above, people poured
into Devlin's for the twenty-five-cent ride.
It looked as though Beach's plan was going
to work.

But **WAIT!**

Some folks weren't so sure about Beach's BIG idea.

Shopkeepers wanted their customers to stay ABOVE the ground.

Property owners worried that all that tunneling might not be good for their buildings.

Others wondered if it might give Beach too much power.

And remember BOSS TWEED? Well, by now, some of his friends had come
up with their own plan for a railroad, and Tweed looked out for his friends.
He wasn't going to let some CRACKPOT inventor cut into their business.

The governor denied Beach's request to expand.

SCREECH! The underground train was stopped in its tracks.

As time passed and the train didn't go any farther, the city's curiosity wore off and the stream of visitors slowed to a drip.

Deep down in the quiet heart of the city, away from the clattering and clanging above, Beach turned off the great fan and sighed. Oh, well. There would be other ideas. But he had shown New York that one day people might move beneath the streets—as if by magic.

By 1874, the train that went nowhere had closed. Beach rented out the tunnel as a shooting gallery, and eventually it was abandoned altogether. It might even have been forgotten.

But many years later, drilling could be heard once again under the streets of New York City. Another underground train, run on electricity, was being built. Workers found lots of surprises as they tunneled: a sunken ship beneath the Battery, mastodon bones near Dyckman Street, subterranean streams in Midtown, and quicksand, not far from City Hall.

And in February 1912, forty-two years after Beach
unveiled his train, they ran into a brick wall.

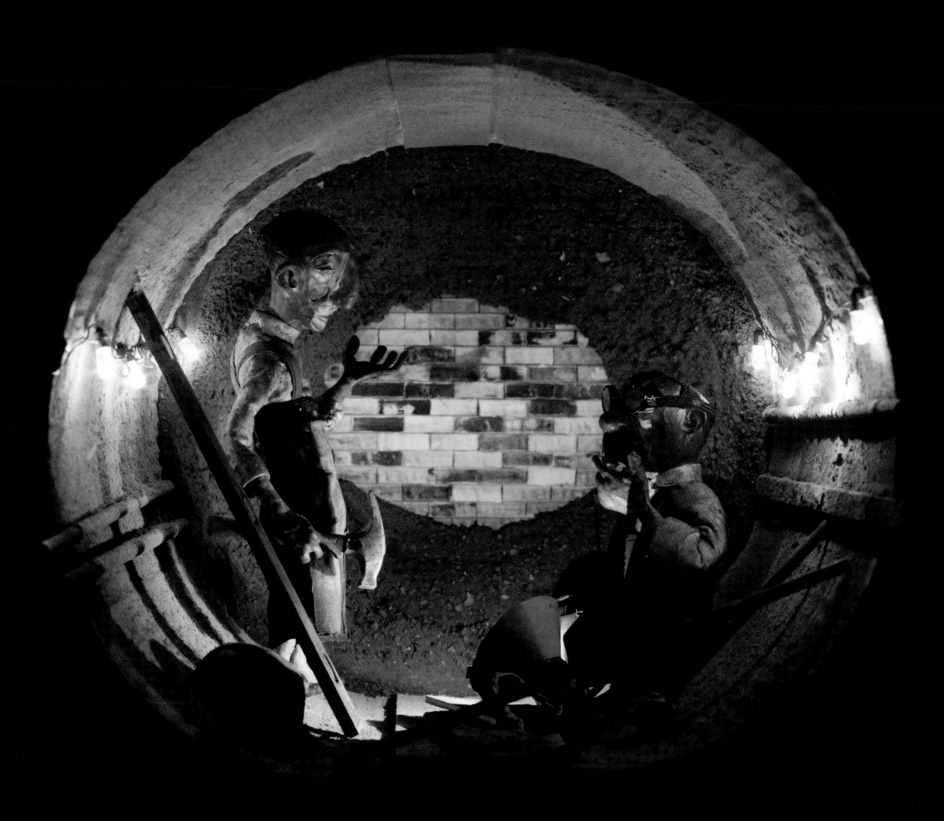

When the workers broke through, they found themselves inside Beach's tunnel. There was even a little railroad car rusting in its tracks, and a tunneling machine perched at the end—

ready to lead the way forward.

Author's Note

Born in Springfield, Massachusetts, in 1826, Alfred Ely Beach grew up to become co-owner and coeditor of *Scientific American* magazine. Although he didn't invent pneumatic power—the power to move things with air pressure (pneumatic tubes had already been used in London to move mail)—he did plan to use it to solve New York City's traffic crisis. Beach introduced his idea at New York's American Institute Fair in 1867, where he exhibited both a small pneumatic tube for carrying packages and a larger tube, suspended from the ceiling, that contained a working passenger railway. The railway was the hit of the fair.

Obtaining permission to build such a railway under the streets of New York City was a process so mired in politics that Beach decided to go around the legal system. After his success at the fair, he received permission to build two small pneumatic mail tubes. He began building them, but he also built a working subway that ran between Warren and Murray Streets in lower Manhattan.

There is some controversy about what happened next. William M. Tweed was the boss of New York's Tammany Hall political machine and, according to legend, was responsible for the derailment of Beach's train. Recent research suggests that the story is more complicated than that, however, and that Tweed started out supporting Beach before ultimately throwing his support behind a plan backed by a bigger player.

department store owner A. T. Stewart. After several more tries and the fall of the Tweed Ring, Beach did eventually get his charter. But the financial panic of 1873 hit, and Beach's funding dried up.

Meanwhile, New York's traffic problems only grew worse. For many years, herds of pigs, sheep, and other animals were driven through New York's streets on the way to slaughter. This was outlawed in 1869, but was a part of the street chaos while Beach planned his subway. There was a whole team of police officers, called the Broadway squad, whose job was to escort people safely across Broadway. And the Brooklyn Dodgers, one of the city's baseball teams, were at one time called the Trolley Dodgers.

The city tried to build an elevated train. But by the turn of the century, New York was looking once again to what were now called subways. New York City's subway wasn't America's first (that honor belongs to Boston, where underground trains began running in 1897), but on March 24, 1900, the city broke ground and a workforce made up mostly of immigrants began building what would become known as the world's greatest subway system.

The first official New York City subway line opened on October 27, 1904, and New Yorkers have been riding the system ever since. With 468 stations and over 650 miles of track, the New York subway takes millions of people where they want to go every day. Alfred Ely Beach would have been proud.

Beach died in 1896. His tunnel was destroyed while building the current system, but the memory of his magical subway station still exists, buried beneath our feet as we walk the city's sidewalks, halfway between its past and its future.

I did most of my research with primary source documents. You can find many of the original newspaper articles from the 1870s, as well as period photographs and Beach's promotional pamphlets about his subway, gathered here: nycsubway.org

And if you're in New York, you can learn more about the subway (and even climb aboard a historic subway car!) at the New York Transit Museum (mta.info/mta/museum) or visit the museum online to find activities and more (transitmuseumeducation.org).

Selected Bibliography

Brennan, Joseph. *Beach Pneumatic: Alfred Beach's Pneumatic Subway and the Beginnings of Rapid Transit in New York.* http://www.columbia.edu/~brennan/beach/.

Cudahy, Brian J. *Under the Sidewalks of New York: The Story of the Greatest Subway System in the World.* 2nd rev. ed. New York: Fordham University Press, 1995.

Hood, Clifton. *722 Miles: The Building of the Subways and How They Transformed New York.* Baltimore: Johns Hopkins University Press, 1993.

"Illustrated Description of the Broadway Pneumatic Underground Railway." New York: S. W. Green, 1870.

Internet Sources

nycsubway.org

Several lines of dialogue have been invented to illustrate political debates of the time. Other quotes were drawn from the following:

"You are respectfully . . .": "The Pneumatic Tube: Reception Under Broadway," *New York Evening Post*, February 26, 1870.

"Remarkable": "The Pneumatic Tunnel Under Broadway," *Scientific American*, March 5, 1870.

"The Railroad of the Future": "The Greatest of Our Bores," *New York Sunday-Mercury*, February 27, 1870.

"The problem of . . .": "The Great Bore," *New York Evening Mail*, February 26, 1870.

For Jack, Nate, and Adelaide. And in memory of
Caleb Mazal Hollander Sande, who loved the subway. —S.C.

To my family, who light the way as I tunnel
and toil with my work. —R.N.S.

ACKNOWLEDGMENTS

My heartfelt thanks to Robert Hayes, librarian (and microfilm expert)
at Brooklyn's Central Library; Robin Nagle, anthropologist-in-residence for the
New York City Department of Sanitation; Tracey Adams at Adams Literary; and to all
my friends at Random House, especially the extraordinary Anne Schwartz and Lee Wade,
who not only welcomed me aboard but also gave me the map and showed me the way. —S.C.

All rights reserved. Published in the United States
by Schwartz & Wade Books, an imprint of Random House
Children's Books, a division of Penguin Random House LLC, New York.
Schwartz & Wade Books and the colophon are trademarks of Penguin Random House LLC.

Visit us on the Web! randomhousekids.com
Educators and librarians, for a variety of teaching tools,
visit us at RHTeachersLibrarians.com

Library of Congress Cataloging-in-Publication Data
Corey, Shana.
The secret subway / Shana Corey ; Red Nose Studio. — First edition.
pages cm
Summary: "In 1870, Alfred Ely Beach invents
New York's first underground train"—Provided by publisher.
Includes bibliographical references.
ISBN 978-0-375-87071-2 (hc) — ISBN 978-0-375-97071-9 (glb) — ISBN 978-0-307-97457-0 (ebook)
1. Subways—New York (State)—New York—History—Juvenile literature. 2. Beach, Alfred E.
(Alfred Ely), 1826–1896—Juvenile literature. I. Red Nose Studio. II. Title.
TF847.N5C66 2016
388.4'2097471—dc23
2014025770

The text of this book is set in Bodoni Old Face.
The illustrations are hand-built three-dimensional sets shot with a Canon EOS 5D Mark III Digital
SLR camera. The line art was drawn with Hunt 108 pen nibs and Higgins Black Magic ink on paper.
The title lettering is inverted blue pencil on paper.
MANUFACTURED IN CHINA
2 4 6 8 10 9 7 5 3 1
First Edition

Random House Children's Books supports the First Amendment and celebrates the right to read.